It's Fun To Be A
Mom

BECKY FREEMAN JOHNSON

HARVEST HOUSE PUBLISHERS

EUGENE, OREGON

Unless otherwise indicated, all Scripture quotations are taken from the HOLY BIBLE, NEW INTERNATIONAL VERSION®. NIV®. Copyright © 1973, 1978, 1984 by the International Bible Society. Used by permission of Zondervan. All rights reserved.

Verses marked TLB are taken from *The Living Bible,* Copyright © 1971. Used by permission of Tyndale House Publishers, Inc., Wheaton, IL 60189 USA. All rights reserved.

Verses marked NASB are taken from the New American Standard Bible®, © 1960, 1962, 1963, 1968, 1971, 1972, 1973, 1975, 1977, 1995 by The Lockman Foundation. Used by permission. (www.Lockman.org)

Verses marked NCV are taken from *The Holy Bible, New Century Version,* Copyright © 1987, 1988, 1991 by Word Publishing, Nashville, TN 37214. Used by permission.

Verses marked NKJV are taken from the New King James Version. Copyright ©1982 by Thomas Nelson, Inc. Used by permission. All rights reserved.

Verses marked KJV are taken from the King James Version of the Bible.

Becky Freeman Johnson: Published in association with the literary agency of WordServe Literary Group, Ltd., 10152 S. Knoll Circle, Highlands Ranch, CO 80130

Every effort has been made to give proper credit for all stories, poems, and quotations. If for any reason proper credit has not been given, please notify the author or publisher and proper notation will be given on future printing.

Cover by Jeff Franke Design and Illustration

Cover photo © Tim Hall / Photodisc Red / Getty Images

IT'S FUN TO BE A MOM

Copyright © 2007 by Becky Freeman Johnson
Published by Harvest House Publishers
Eugene, Oregon 97402
www.harvesthousepublishers.com

Library of Congress Cataloging-in-Publication Data
Johnson, Becky Freeman, 1959-
It's fun to be a mom / Becky Freeman Johnson.
   p. cm.
ISBN-13: 978-0-7369-1803-9
ISBN-10: 0-7369-1803-5
1. Mothers--Religious life. I. Title.
BV4529.18.J632 2007
242'.6431--dc22

                                                                        2006016227

Printed in China

        07 08 09 10 11 12 13 / RDS-CF / 10 9 8 7 6 5 4 3 2 1

To my mother, Ruthie Arnold,
who wrote down all the cute and
funny things we did as kids.
When I became a mother, I followed her lead.
Who would have dreamed those notes
on napkins and backs of envelopes
would someday become a book,
and another, and another…

Thank you, Mother, for teaching me
how to love, laugh, and write.
They say that we write to "taste life twice."

Because of your fabulous mothering
and literary mentoring,
I have been doubly blessed.

Acknowledgments

First I have to thank my four kids—Zach, Zeke, Rachel Praise, and Gabe—for making me such a proud and happy mama, and for being so generous with the material of their lives. Now that you are all grown-up, you've also had a taste of role reversal—of comforting and advising me through valley days and rejoicing with me as our lives have settled back onto a lovely mountaintop. One of life's great surprises is to look at your adult children and realize that you've just raised yourself a great bunch of supportive friends.

Second, my heartfelt gratitude to the folks at Harvest House Publishers—particularly Bob Hawkins Jr., Terry Glaspey, Carolyn McCready, and LaRae Weikert—for not just talking about grace but for actually being "God's love with skin on" to me when my life, as I knew it, blew into so many pain-filled pieces. Thank you from the depths of my soul for reminding me of who I am and trusting me to continue sharing my heart through the written word. Thanks to the ever-encouraging and talented Jean Christen and Kim Moore for doing the fine-tuning on this manuscript.

Last, but certainly not least, I want to thank the love of my life, my husband, Greg Johnson, for putting me back together again; for loving me truly, deeply, madly every blessed day of my life. Your kind and tender "husbanding" has created the garden from which I've been able to blossom into an ecstatically happy wife, serene mother, and more creative writer. Not only that, but you've shared your wonderful sons, Drew and Troy, with me too, giving me even more blessings to love.

Oh, and you just happen to be the world's best literary agent.

I love you so.

Contents

Note to Readers

When going back into my memory for stories of birthing and raising my now-grown children, I could not do so without occasionally referring to Scott, my then-husband and the father of my children. Scott was, and is, a great dad. We love our children and the good memories of raising them together in Texas.

Sorrowfully, a few years ago our marriage came to an end. For those of you who have read my books in the past and wondered if I disappeared—well, for a while I truly felt that I did. Divorce leaves one wondering who you are for a very long time. Out of respect for our grown kids who love us both, I've chosen to not write about the details of our marriage's unraveling. The worst of that painful season is over, and what matters most to all of us is that we continue to cherish the memories behind us, love and forgive each other today, and smile at the future before us.

Happily, God is the author of second chances, and I was

amazingly blessed to find love again and become Mrs. Greg Johnson in 2004. Troy and Drew, Greg's grown sons, have made my new role as stepmom as enjoyable and easy a transition as any new wife could imagine. We live in Colorado today, and at this writing, five out of six of our adult children (and their mates), plus a brand new grandson, live nearby. (We're working on luring my daughter, Rachel, to the mountains, but she has a great job and an even better man that are keeping her Texas-bound for now.)

My role as mom today has simply expanded as there are more family members to love. For true love never divides; it only multiplies. I often tell people I feel like one of those Italian mamas in the movies, with people of all ages and personalities wandering in and out of the kitchen for a hot meal, a warm hug, coffee cup conversation, or the latest funny story. (And, of course, there's my newlywed husband wandering in to kiss the cook with great regularity.)

In short, the laughter is back. It's wonderful to be in a place where I can once again peck out stories I hope will bring you a smile, and along with that smile, hope.

Becky Freeman Johnson

1

Perchance, to Dance?

Love, like bread, must be made new every day.
OLD SWEDISH SAYING

was heading out the door of a country-style restaurant complete with a Western swing band and a sawdust covered dance floor. As I neared the back of the room, the lyrics of the beautiful love song the band was playing waltzed through my mind, "Yes, you look wonderful tonight." I turned my head just in time to see a young couple with a "Do you remember romance?" look in their weary eyes. The woman's hair was disheveled, and her blouse had the telltale signs of baby spit-up on the right shoulder. He was in a plain T-shirt, jean shorts, and sandals. Between them was an infant seat overflowing with about 15 pounds of adorable baby boy.

Apparently the waitress had observed the same scene. I watched as she walked up to the couple and asked, "Would you like to dance to this song?" The young mother nodded, and for a moment I thought she might cry. The young man choked out, "This was our wedding song." The little waitress in blue jeans and gingham said, "Well, ya'll go on out there and DANCE! Don't worry. I'll watch the baby for you. Have fun."

I walked over to the waitress and said, "That was the sweetest thing I've observed in a long time. How did you know that young couple wanted to dance?"

She just smiled as she bounced the baby and said, "After you work here a while, you get to know the look between a husband and wife that says, 'They're playing our song.' I saw The Look and knew they needed a chance to dance."

The young husband slipped his arm around his wife's waist, and I wiped at a tear as I watched them change from parents into lovers in one measure of a love song and one turn on the dance floor.

There's nothing more uniting—or dividing—to a marriage than the birth of children. My heart always goes out to the exhausted and nurturing new mother, and equally to the new dad who misses his wife when she is totally preoccupied with a new love in her life. Though it is never easy, and money may be tight, the best investment you can make in your future as a couple is to make time and allow a budget for a regular weekly date night. Then promise yourselves to take every little chance you get to keep your romance alive—whether it be a kiss over the highchair or a waltz across the kitchen floor. Even if you have to wipe spit-up off your shoulder or step over a pile of diapers to do so.

I am my lover's and my lover is mine.

Song of Songs 6:3

2

Dreamin' of a Full Night's Sleep

Small children disturb your sleep, big children your life.

<small>YIDDISH PROVERB</small>

I love the story about a little boy, a summer evening, and a violent thunderstorm. His mother was tucking him into bed and was about to turn off the light when he asked with a tremor in his voice, "Mommy, will you sleep with me tonight?"

The mother smiled and gave her small son a reassuring hug. "I can't, dear," she said. "I have to sleep in Daddy's room."

A long silence was broken at last by his shaky little voice. "The big sissy."

This bedtime anecdote reminded me of our own bedtime struggles with our children. Out of empathy and pity, we'd allowed our kids to waddle into our room in the middle of the night whenever they grew lonely or afraid. (Or hungry or thirsty or bored or…) But after we added a few more children to our brood, my husband and I realized we were no longer sleeping through the night; we were EXPERIENCING it. When we were reduced to sleeping on mattress spaces the size of tea towels, we knew something had to be done. Something involving getting the kids out of our bed before we went out of our minds.

The first night after our resolve, Zachary—about age four—toddled into our room and began his automatic sleep-climbing into our bed. Though I was groggy, I got up, took his hand, and led him back to his own room. Needless to say, Zach was not pleased with this new arrangement. I reached for a large stuffed bear and snuggled it next to him, tucking them both under a quilt.

"There," I said soothingly. "You have a nice big Pooh Bear to sleep with now."

Without missing a beat, Zach took one look at the bear and then turned his puppy-brown eyes toward mine and said, "I'd rather have a nice big Mommy."

My sister, Rachel, related a similar bedtime revelation that occurred to her son, Trevor, when she wrote me the following in a letter.

> Dear Becky,
> The other night we were exhausted with our efforts to get Trev to stay in his bed. We'd bought him a Power Ranger bedspread and matching

sheets and given him all kinds of bedtime toys to play with, but no matter what we did he wouldn't stay put. Finally I asked, "What's WRONG with your bed?" Trevor looked at us like, duh, we should KNOW what's wrong with it. Holding both hands toward the empty bed in exasperation he said, "There's no people in it!"

When is that turnabout when we start to enjoy, even savor rather than dread, going to bed? For me, it occurred when my children grew older and the nighttime ordeal became, mercifully, less traumatic.

When my kids were quite tiny, we had such an involved pre-bedtime routine. I read to them, bathed them, rocked them, sang to them, prayed with them, nursed or watered them, diapered or pottied them, bear-hugged them, kissed them, and stopped often to gaze at them—cute as a basket of baby bunnies in pastel feety pajamas. Then I repeated many of these things several more times throughout the evening before they actually fell asleep. By that time I was wiped out—too exhausted even to cry, much less marvel over how cute they were.

Then came the long-awaited day when my kids-turned-teens often came to find *me* to say their goodnights, tucking me, as it were, into bed. They actually bathed themselves, poured their own drinks of water, and turned out their own lights. Heaven! Of course, there were also those late night vigils when my key-toting, car-driving, hormone-induced kids were out too late for my peace of mind. Then I struggled with visions of them gone over a cliff or wrapped around a tree until, at last, I heard the front door open, and—joy!—the sound of them padding quietly down the hall, hoping not to disturb me.

And now…the house is emptied of children altogether. No bedtime hassles, no late night worries, just a hot bubble bath all to myself (unless I share it with my husband), a good book, and a cup of chamomile tea.

But what I wouldn't give to see my babies, once more, cute as a basket of baby bunnies snuggled up in their feety pajamas.

For he grants sleep to those he loves.

PSALM 127:2

3

Mammeries Are
Made of This

*To have my baby take nourishment from my
body, to see his eyes drift shut, to hear his
purring contentment, is painfully exquisite.*

JUDITH GEISSLER

put the diaper bag down on the floor beside me with a sigh.
My newborn son, wrapped in a blanket as soft as blue sky, was
sleepily nuzzling my neck. I prayed he'd hold off for just a few
minutes more before he demanded I serve up his mid-morning
snack of milk and schnookies.

Glancing around the living room full of new mommies, I
immediately began to feel comforted. Clearly, I wasn't alone in my

struggles adapting to mommyhood. Our eyes were all drooping from lack of sleep, the fragrance of "Eau de Last Spit-Up" drifted from our shoulders, and the telltale mark of every nursing mother decorated our blouses: Two wet coaster-shaped circles, marking the place where normal breasts once abided.

Since giving birth to a child, we'd all marveled at the twin watermelon-sized feeding bags that swelled from our respective chests. Almost overnight we'd gone from being shapely, attractive women to your basic herd of Jerseys, with parachute-sized bras drying over our shower curtain rods.

Now all we had left were mammaries…er, memories…of our less-than-missile-sized busts.

Here at La Leche League, we weekly turned to each other for affirmation and reminders of why we were choosing to breast-feed our offspring. (Actually, to avoid having to shout over two sets of burgeoning busts, we stood side by side.) We were a support group of bushed, big-bosom buddies.

One mother sighed as she piped up. "I feel like an unattractive hybrid of Dolly Parton and Quasimodo—leaning forward from this ponderous 'mother load.' I've contemplated stealing a grocery cart so I can slide these things into the leg holes of the kid seat and strap 'em in."

Laughter exploded around the room as bombs of relief and empathy went off from every corner.

"The other morning," I chimed in, "I woke up so full of milk that when I turned over, a stream of breast milk arched across the bed and hit the window. 'Nice shot,' my husband deadpanned. 'Now see if you can hit that fly over there.'"

Again the laughter, and with it the atmosphere lightened

some more. We were now, so to speak, milking our predicament for all it was worth.

"The worst part for me," a redheaded mother explained, "is when my husband comes home and asks me what I've done. I say something like, 'I made half of the bed and then nursed the baby. I combed half of my hair and then nursed the baby. I got half dressed and then nursed the baby. I made it through half the day and fell asleep in the rocker, nursing the baby.' I've been reduced to a rocking human feeding tube."

"Then why," I asked incredulously, "are we DOING THIS?"

"Well…it's good for the baby," one mother reminded us as she burped her infant and deftly handed her toddler a Tippy Cup in one swift motion.

"Nothing is as nutritious as mother's milk, you know," said a full-time mommy and former pediatric nurse.

"And it's more convenient than bottles and nipples and formula and stuff."

At this point in the conversation, I had to mentally check out. Baby Zach was beginning to wiggle and protest. Enough was enough. He'd chewed on my empty neck bone all he was going to chew without a food-based reward for his efforts. It was time for the real thing.

As I watched him hungrily, frantically, wiggle his downy head back and forth in a desperate search for the source of all comfort, the elixir of life, I could not restrain a smile. Tiny hands, twin pieces of living art, reached toward me, squeezing and patting my skin as if in gratitude. Then, snagging a strand of my dark hair, he twisted it round and round in complete fascination at what he had caught. Two ebony eyes searched for mine, caught my gaze, and held it.

I could see my face reflected in those dark baby pools.

And what I saw was unconditional love.

As I glanced up, I saw mother after mother put baby to breast in a ritual of love as old as humankind. Though we complained about the inconveniences involved in caring for infants, grieved the losses of our once firm figures, and whined about the absence of visible productivity—in our hearts, we knew the truth.

Rarely would we ever again do anything as profoundly important as this nourishing of new life, straight from the hand of heaven.

♡ ♡ ♡

*You made me trust in you even
at my mother's breast.*

Psalm 22:9

4

A Typical Day in the Life of a Mommy

If it were going to be easy, it never would have started with something called labor.

AUTHOR UNKNOWN

7:00 AM—Awakened with a gentle tap-tap-tap by a small sticky hand on your sleep-laden eyelids. Gingerly, you open one eye. Though the scene is a little fuzzy, you can make out one toddler in feety pajamas holding a jar of grape jelly to his chest with his left hand, patting you tenderly with his dimpled, jelly-coated right hand.

You smile weakly as child asks you to get up and help him find the peanut butter.

8:00 AM—Having downed a cup of coffee, you are now standing at the mirror, bearing only a vague resemblance to your former Before-Kids Self, and removing grape jelly pats from various and sundry parts of your body. Toddler is wailing in a time-out for throwing a rabid fit when you cut his peanut butter and jelly toast diagonally instead of up and down. You estimate the remainder of his time-out, wondering if it's safe to risk taking a quick bath. You remember those halcyon days when drawing a hot bubble bath signaled anticipated time alone, not an invitation to a hot tub party for mom and tot.

11:00 AM—You are looking, in vain, for a pound of hamburger you were sure was thawing on the kitchen counter. You check on toddler playing in the sandbox outside and see him holding the pound of hamburger by one end and giggling at the kitty cat that is happily gorging himself on the unexpected treat at the other end.

1:00 PM—You read *Pat the Bunny* six times, until finally, blessedly, toddler falls asleep. Tiptoeing out of the room, you glance back at child's long lashes, his little round tummy rising and falling with each breath, and dash back to kiss his soft cheek. Then you toss a mental coin: *Do I take a nap or clean the house that is falling down around my ears?* You yawn and sink down beside resting child, curling your body around his, and give in to the undertow of sleep.

3:00 PM—On a walk to the park you answer 76 questions, all beginning with "Why," "What," or "How." You are a walking encyclopedia of Things Toddlers Want to Know, such as: "Why Some Worms Wear Sweaters" and "Why Fingers Gots Two

Elbows." Forget *Who Wants to Be a Millionaire?* They need a game show called *Who Wants to Be a Mommy?* It takes more stamina and scientific knowledge, and it requires gargantuan nerves of steel.

5:00 PM—You make a stab at cleaning the house and then open a can of SpaghettiOs for dinner (since your child made sure Kitty enjoyed tonight's original entrée). You hear a loud, clattering noise—a noise you've come to dread. Toddler has managed to pull toy box into the kitchen and dump contents on the tile floor. Again. You wonder how he gets the strength to haul a toy box from room to room but goes weak-kneed and limp when required to pick up one plastic Lego block.

7:30 PM—Husband comes home, surveys the damage a two-foot-high child can do to a 2000 square foot house in the course of a day, looks hopefully toward the kitchen stove, frowns, and asks, "So tell me, what did you do all day?"

Can you relate, Moms? I loved the following, forwarded from an Internet buddy, written by Ken Davis.

> Have you heard about the next planned *Survivor* show?
>
> Six men will be dropped on an island with one van and four kids each for six weeks. Here are the challenges:
>
> - Each kid plays two sports and either takes music or dance classes.
>
> - There is no access to fast food.
>
> - Each man must take care of his four kids, keep his assigned house clean, correct all homework, complete science projects, cook, do laundry, etc.

- There is only one TV between them and no remote.

- The men only have access to television when the kids are asleep and all chores are done.

- The men must shave their legs and wear makeup daily, which they must apply themselves either while driving or while making four lunches.

- They must attend weekly PTA meetings; clean up after their sick children at three AM; make an Indian hut model with six toothpicks, a tortilla, and one Magic Marker; and get a four-year-old to eat a serving of peas.

- The kids vote them off based on performance. The winner gets to go back to his job.

Come unto me all you who are weary and burdened, and I will give you rest.

MATTHEW 11:28

5

Critter Kid

Little kids are really weird, aren't they?
GABRIEL FREEMAN, AGE 16, OBSERVING HIS YOUNGER COUSINS

Some mothers of preschoolers use TV as a babysitter. Not me. No, sir. The first thing every morning when my three-year-old lastborn awoke, I'd run outside our lakeside home, look for any small creature that was breathing and moving, pop it in an empty butter tub, poke holes in it (the tub, not the critter), and Gabriel was set for the day.

There were days, however, when I probably should have fallen back on the reliability of *Sesame Street.* One such day began as I sat folding the morning's wash. I noticed, with a sense of unease, a strange bulge in the pocket of a pair of Gabe's jeans. Gingerly,

I forced myself to explore the warm, dark interior of the pocket, reminded of the feeling I'd had years before when the bigger neighborhood kids would blindfold us little kids and force us to stick our hands into a bowl of cooked spaghetti (all the while assuring us the bowl contained either brains or guts). I realized, as I explored the pocket under discussion, that I hadn't matured all that much.

My hand closed around an object that could have been a piece of bark. Feeling false reassurance, I extracted the mysterious bulge. Can anyone know how black and shriveled and, well, bark-like a frog can be unless they have seen one washed, rinsed, and fluff-dried?

Toward evening that same day, things quieted down entirely too long. (Have you ever wondered why six minutes of peace feed the soul of a toddler's mother, while seven fill it with terror?) On the seventh minute I dropped my chopping knife with a clatter and ran out to the back porch to check on Gabriel. All was strangely calm. In fact, he seemed to be meditating, his gaze fixed upon a Styrofoam ice chest waiting to be stored away. Our eyes met when I heard a thumping sound issuing from the closed ice chest.

"There's a cat in there," Gabe said matter-of-factly, jerking his thumb toward the chest. I was not unduly alarmed for the safety of the cat at this point, since I could see the lid of the chest rise and fall with the thumps, but I did move to liberate the animal. As I lifted the lid, I realized with shock that Gabe had managed to fill the chest with water before depositing Kitty. I grabbed the saturated feline by her neck and estimated her to be on about her ninth life. I turned horrified eyes on my son. Like George Washington, he did not lie.

"I put her in there," he confessed. But he had a reason. "She was really thirsty."

At one time I thought my life as the mother of a critter-loving kid would never come to an end. Trust me, there's no experience to compare with downing the last of a big glass of iced tea only to discover a grayish worm squirming among the cubes at the bottom. "Just look, " Gabe had cooed sweetly as he showed me a pail of sand containing a number of worms he had not yet invited to tea. "See how they love each other? They're hugging!"

Today my critter-lovin' baby is a tall, dark, handsome young man. Snails, pails, and box turtle tails have been replaced by girls, loud music, and basketball. But sometimes Gabe will walk into the kitchen, lean over the counter, and say, "I love you, Mom."

In those rare moments, I can still see a little bit of the boy who used to surprise me with slime-covered snails—and I reach out to hug him tightly. And sometimes we just stand there in the kitchen, happily hugging for a couple of seconds—mother and son. Just like a couple of contented worms.

My command is this: Love each other as I have loved you.

JOHN 15:12

6

It's Mom's Turn for a Hug

To understand a parent's love, have a child.
JAPANESE PROVERB

Now that my children are grown, one might think I've forgotten what it was like to be a mother of small children. Let me just say this once, very plainly: I WILL NEVER FORGET. And I will never judge a mother of small children. If she is still standing by the end of a long week with toddlers, she deserves a medal in my book. I know what she needs from me, for I was once her for many years.

In fact, let's say that one day, as I sit typing this book in delicious peace (all my now-grown children tucked away at school, work, or college), there is a knock at my front door.

I stroll to open it and gasp at the sight. On the porch stands an obviously frazzled woman at the end of her mental rope. Her eyes are red-rimmed with tears and sleep deprivation, the hem of her denim skirt has the telltale signs of small peanut butter handprints, and two round wet spots on her blouse indicate the overflow of a nursing mother. In hands that have not seen a manicure in months, she clutches a small red suitcase. (It says "Going to Grandma's" in bright cartoon letters.) There's a cardboard sign around her neck (dangling from a necklace made with yarn and Fruit Loops) whose hand-scrawled letters read, "Will Beg for One Hour's Peace." Weakly, she manages to say, "I'm a mother of small children and, frankly, I just can't take it anymore. I'm running away from home! Can you help me?"

"Say no more," I tell her soothingly, reaching out to pull her into my arms and then into my kitchen for a hot cup of tea (with nary a cracker crumb or Cocoa Puff floating on top).

This mother doesn't need a lecture on child psychology; she doesn't need a 365-page parenting manual. She needs a nap. She needs some love. She needs some encouragement and refreshment. After her most immediate needs are tended to, maybe we'll chat about practical ways to better love, nurture, and discipline her children. But just as the flight attendant always tells parents to put on their oxygen masks before helping their children with theirs, a mom needs to attend to her needs so she can attend to the needs of her kids.

An oft-neglected truth for caretakers of small children is this: The first order of business MUST be to nurture the nurturer as often as possible. For as my friend Lindsey O'Connor's book title says, *If Mama Ain't Happy, Ain't Nobody Happy.*

What are some ways to fill up your empty cup? Here are a few ideas to get you started. Enjoy!

1. Make sure you get one day a week completely to yourself with a good Mother's Day Out program or exchange a Mom's Day Off with another mom.

2. Instead of mopping the floor, let it go one more day and pamper yourself during your child's naptime. Put on soft music, light a candle, take a hot bath, read a mindless magazine. You will be so renewed, you may even tackle that floor later on while you make a game of it with your child!

3. Have lunch without kids once every two weeks with a funny and interesting friend. Make sure you use at least every other Mother's Day Out as a purely FUN day, and not just a day to catch up on errands.

4. Do whatever it takes to have a regular date night with your husband. There are no good excuses for not doing this. Babysitting can be exchanged. There are plenty of books and creative ideas for free or nearly free date nights with your mate—from window-shopping to making out like teenagers in the back of your minivan in a grocery store parking lot. It's your love life. Without it things get very dangerous in a marriage. Soooo…JUST DO IT. You'll never be sorry.

Come with me by yourselves to a
quiet place and get some rest.

Mark 6:31

7

Precious in Pink

Sugar and spice and everything nice,
that's what little girls are made of.

OLD NURSERY RHYME

My sister, Rachel, had just given birth to her second child in eight years. My nephew, Trevor, an only child for so long, was now big brother to a baby sister. So I drove from a speaking engagement in North Carolina to Atlanta (where Rachel lived at the time) to hold Tori Leigh, all seven pounds, seven ounces of miracle-in-the-flesh. Mother had landed in town just a couple of hours before Rachel went into labor and was there in the delivery room when Tori made her grand debut. Mother gave a blow-by-blow (or push-by-push) account to my father through her cell phone. Later my father told me, "I didn't think I'd get emotional, but, Becky, when I heard Rachel's baby girl cry over that cell phone, I cried right along with her."

I'd been worried about Mother making the trip to Atlanta—her heart had been acting up a bit before the impending birth of her grandchild. Just before I took off for North Carolina, I called her and said, "Mother, if you need to have surgery or anything, no matter how busy I am, I will halt everything to be with you. I want you to know that I'll move in with you and cook and clean and be your nursemaid…"

But before I could even finish my sentence, Mother answered, with intense feeling behind every word, "Oh, Becky, dear. You have no idea how motivating that is for me to stay well." I knew then that my quick-witted mother would be fine. For whatever might be ailing us, humor, along with prayer and friends, always promotes a cure. (One of my favorite sayings among the females in our family is "We may have dysfunctions, but we at least have the decency to make them sound entertaining.")

When I arrived at Rachel's apartment, the first crisp nips of fall were playing about the early September air. Only pausing to give quick hugs to mother and to Rachel, I walked straight from the front door to the nursery for a peek at our baby. As imagined, she was perfect. Downy dark hair, rosebud lips. Tiny body, moving in dreamy slow motion, wrapped in an antique rose-covered nightie, seen via the light pouring on her from a nearby window. She looked like a Rembrandt painting. Her fingers were outstretched toward the light, her eyes struggling to open wide like a puppy's to take in the Big World. I'd forgotten how precious is a newborn's small, warm body—the faint scent of baby oil, the silky softness of her skin touching my cheek.

Mother looked on at her two daughters, Rachel and me, and at her new granddaughter—the only girl to arrive in our family since my daughter, Rachel Praise, had been born nearly 17 years ago. Love and joy and a sense of all-rightness surrounded us.

Small, ordinary things—a meal shared, a diaper changed, a baby bath, a game played—all seemed extra special. A new baby in the house adds a certain glow to what could seem mundane. That evening Trevor and his daddy and my mother asked me to join them in a domino game of 42. It was a rousing fun game, although I admit I was a little distracted by the warmth and snuggling of my niece lying half-awake in my arms as I played my hand. Halfway through the game, Trevor asked, "Um, Aunt Becky. I'd kind of like to win a game now. Would you mind if you be my dad's partner so I can have Granny for mine?" Mother just beamed. I did the only mature thing a grown daughter could do in admitting defeat to her sweet mother. I stuck my tongue out at her.

The next morning I awoke to share one last coffee moment over breakfast with Mother and Rach before flying home to Texas. I took a bite of warm cinnamon toast and a swallow of Folgers. "Hey, Rachel, remember how you wanted another boy?"

She nodded.

"I know you've always been kind of a tomboy, and I know how much you've enjoyed Trevor and his friends," I said with empathy, "but I couldn't help praying all these years that God would give you a daughter as well."

Mother nodded her agreement.

My sister looked over at her daughter, sucking happily on her miniature fingers—a little doll-baby wrapped in a cloud of soft pink.

"I think I'll keep her," she said, bending over to kiss Tori's downy head. "I've decided a daughter was what I wanted after all."

Just before I left I took pictures of mother and Rachel and baby Tori. They'll go into a scrapbook, and in about 20 years Tori will be flipping through the yellowing pages and pointing and oohing and aahing and dreaming of the day when she'll become a mother, like her own mother and Aunt Becky and Granny Ruthie and Nonnie before her.

Because the love and laughter and dreams of the females in our family tree are really what little girls are made of.

Many daughters have done well,
but you excel them all.

PROVERBS 31:29 NKJV

8

Becky's Helpful Household Hints

Dishes and dusting can wait till tomorrow,
For children grow up, I've learned to my sorrow.
So quiet down, cobwebs, and, dust, go to sleep.
I'm rocking my baby, and babies don't keep.

AUTHOR UNKNOWN

Anyone who's read my books or stepped through my front door knows that I will never be asked to be the next Martha Stewart. In fact, Martha Stewart not only doesn't live here, she wouldn't even want to drop by for a quick visit. Even her temporary jail cell, I'm sure, was a step up from my house on a good day, especially when it was filled to the brim with four kids and their various friends. (Though still messy at heart, it is amazing how much cleaner the house stays now that it has only two adults in it.)

And even though I've never had any photographers drop in from *Good Housekeeping* begging to take photos, I've managed to keep my home somewhere above the "Early American Ransacked" look, all while raising a houseful of children, writing more than a dozen books, finding ways to feed and clothe and entertain a family, laughing out loud more times than I can possibly count, and fitting in regular naps. Okay. So I may not have clean socks in my drawers at this moment, but neither do I have a peptic ulcer.

Here's some ways that I, as a type B Mom, managed some household chores through the years.

The Clean Sweep. Quickly getting everything up and out of sight before dinnertime, I often literally swept toys into a closet with a huge broom and shut the door. (Hint: You may have to lean on it really hard.) On my Cheerful Mother days, I'd enlist the kids' help by singing the tidying-up song from *Mary Poppins,* "A Spoonful of Sugar," in my best English nanny soprano. I could also manage a pretty good dwarf imitation for a rousing rendition of "Heigh-ho, heigh-ho! To clean our room we go!" The kids loved it until about age seven, when my singing suddenly embarrassed them. Then I resorted to turning my singing into a threat: "If you don't clean your room, I'm gonna start in with the SHOW TUNES!" This was guaranteed to send them scrambling for a broom and dustpan in record time.

Organize One Drawer or Shelf Per Day. Try tackling short, five-minute tasks to help you feel in control of SOMETHING again since everything else in your world has slipped from your control since the moment you experienced your first hard labor pain. (I know the correct word for "birth pain" is a "contraction." But this is hilariously insane. It's like calling a tsunami a little wave. I pushed all four of my kids into this world via unmedicated home births—in natural, cozy, EXCRUTIATING PAIN. So speak not to me of *contractions,* which sound like some mild uterine squeeze that can be rationalized or negotiated with.)

If your budget will allow it, hire a housekeeper to come in one to four times a month. If housecleaning isn't your thing but money is too scarce for hired help, see if you can trade a day of housecleaning for babysitting, cooking, or running errands, etc. with a neat-freak friend who might actually get some genuine jollies from cleaning your house.

Until you can apply for Meals on Wheels (why doesn't some charity take pity and start this program for young mothers?), the bad news is that not only will you have to raise children and keep the house out of condemned status, you will also have to make dinner for your family. I agree. It seems a bit much to ask of a sleep-deprived, postpartum human, but, alas, we must eat. Start filing recipes that are yummy, easy, and *make you look good* in a folder and keep it handy in the kitchen. (Ask other moms for their top two favorite recipes in this category.) I personally love Liz Curtis Higgs recipe for casseroles in a pinch: "Take everything on the left half of your refrigerator. Combine it with everything on the right half. Sprinkle with potato chips and bake at 350." Enjoy! Not only the casserole, but your life. (And you *will* get one again.)

Keep in mind that you won't be thinking about the condition of your house when you are on your deathbed. You'll remember the love-covered messes that made up the memories you cherish the most.

Look at the birds of the air, they do not sow or reap or stow away in barns, and yet your heavenly Father feeds them. Are you not much more valuable than they?

Matthew 6:26

9

Commonsense Parenting

Even if parents managed to do everything perfectly, they'd still raise little sinners in need of God's grace.

MY MOTHER, RUTHIE ARNOLD

A few years ago I was asked to emcee, Oprah-style, a very interesting evening at Illinois State University. The event was sponsored by the large hospital in the Normal area. On the forum that night were two very different child-rearing "experts," presenting two very different ways to raise and discipline children. An obviously conservative couple represented the popular religious-based program *Growing Kids God's Way.* The husband wore a suit, the wife a classic print dress. Their demeanor was kind, relaxed, and controlled. Their children seemed well behaved and happy.

The other presenter was a popular radio psychologist, also a Christian. Very laid-back, fun-loving, high energy. He was dressed in jeans, a casual shirt, and tennis shoes—and he was extolling the virtues of a discipline method called *1-2-3 Magic.* His children seemed well behaved and happy.

My job was to keep the evening light and informative. We were not there to debate.

I was pleased and surprised to see how easy that challenge turned out to be. Both presenters were gracious, both admitting that the method they'd chosen to raise their children worked well, in part, because it was a method they felt most comfortable using for personal reasons.

When it comes to disciplining your children, there are a dozen excellent "methods." Most likely you will end up choosing one that fits your own lifestyle and personality. As long as there is at least as much emphasis on loving your children as there is on correcting and training your children, you and your children will do just fine.

My one heartfelt mothering caution is this: If you find that a certain "method" of disciplining your child is leaving you more and more irritated, frustrated, and angry at your kid's level of performance, if you feel yourself turning into Drill Sergeant Dad or Manic Mom, there is probably an overemphasis on discipline without enough grace, positive reinforcement, humor, and play to balance it all out.

The Old Testament book of Micah tells what God desires: *"He has told you what he wants, and this is all it is: to be fair, just, merciful, and to walk humbly with your God"* (Micah 6:8 TLB).

We are to expect our children to do right. We are to train them to be good and just. But if there is ever a question in your heart when correcting a child, "Is this a time for justice or mercy?" and you sincerely don't know the answer—lean toward mercy. Less permanent mistakes are made, less psychological damage is done from parents who tend to be more grace-oriented than parents who put "behaving right" as the top priority in their home.

We are to be people and parents who require justice, for sure, but we are to be *in love* with the concept of mercy and grace.

For we were once children ourselves, and we made our own little red wagonloads of mistakes. In fact, we are *forever children* to God, our heavenly Father. And aren't you glad He deals with us, most often, according to His grace and mercy, and less often according to what we deserve?

Perhaps this is what Micah means when he says we are to "walk humbly" with our God. The best way to walk humbly is to remember how easily we all fall down.

*Be joyful in hope, patient in
affliction, faithful in prayer.*

Romans 12:12

10

Habits of Highly Real Moms

Real mothers often have sticky floors,
filthy ovens, and happy kids.
AUTHOR UNKNOWN

There are Ideal Moms. I've yet to actually meet one, but I've heard they exist somewhere over the rainbow. Most kids, however, can live very happily with less-than-ideal as long as their mother is real. So, what qualities make a real mother?

Well…

1. She laughs easily. Kids won't remember a spotless house, but they will *always* remember the times when you dropped everything to laugh with them. I used to pretend I was writing a column on the funny things kids do and say, just to keep my sense of humor and sanity. (Tip: Write these things down right away!) Who would have dreamed these scribbled notes from a harried mother would end up as the foundation for a writing and speaking career?

2. She blooms where she's budgeted. When you have young kids and stay at home, money is usually verrrry tight. This can be frustrating, sometimes even embarrassing. I drove an old STATION WAGON (when minivans were what the cool moms drove) for several years because it was cheap (as in "given to us") and held plenty of kids, their accompanying minnow buckets, fishing poles, assorted critters, and wet bathing suits. Be creative—do picnics in the park instead of McDonald's, make your own play dough, shop for resale bargains or garage sale finds. Love, laughter, creativity, and your presence will cover up the shortage of almost all material goods.

3. She tries to find some way to say "I love you" every day. So you might forget to sign their homework papers. Perhaps you sent them to school with two different shoes on their feet. Gave them Frosted Flakes for dinner last night. But if you found a way to tell them you love them, much will be forgiven. Three magic phrases are guaranteed to bring a grin: "I sure do love you, kiddo." "You are my sunshine, did you know that? You bring so much joy to my heart." "I'm so proud of you! Way to go!"

4. She relaxes with her flaws. Remember that the more you relax with your imperfections and theirs, the less the chance you'll raise a little obsessive-compulsive perfectionist. Teach them by modeling that there are some things you don't do very well, but you've learned to ask for help. This gives other people the wonderful chance to feel needed! As mentioned before, if you failed Housekeeping 101, trade housecleaning with some spiffy-clean mom while you babysit her kids or make dinner or wallpaper her bathroom. God makes us all different for a reason. We need each other!

5. She realizes her children are also here to teach her. What mother hasn't secretly wished that she could be the one who got to crawl up in someone else's lap to be held and rocked and loved and soothed? Just as our children reach for our hands in the dark, so we moms—on our own individual dark days—can always revert to being children with God, our Father. In fact, Christ said that to enter His kingdom and all He has for us, there's no other way to come but to run into His arms with the trust of a small child (Matthew 18:3). Children teach us much about God's love that we really can't experience any other way than by becoming a parent.

6. She gathers a circle of support. Young motherhood is the time of life when we most need other friends, particularly other mothers with kids the ages of our children. You can find them at MOPS (Mothers of Preschoolers) groups at churches, Mom and Tot classes at the YMCA, and collapsed in exhaustion on small tables at fast-food playgrounds. Put in the effort it takes to gather a group of three or four fun moms that meets on a weekly basis to share ideas, frustrations, prayers, and funny stories. You might, as a group, decide to trade babysitting nights one month, bake double batches of freezable casseroles or goodies together while the kids play, or take the kids on a field trip to the zoo. Moms need moms to keep from feeling isolated and overwhelmed.

I highly recommend that mothers take advantage of Mother's Day Out programs. If your group of fun moms uses the same Mother's Day Out, you can go out together for a girlfriend lunch or get a makeover together. Or have a book club afternoon. MOPS groups offer programs to encourage moms, and they often offer an extra two to three hours of babysitting so you can go to lunch (check out www.mops.org).

7. She gives her kids a hope-filled vision of the future. Limit TV watching—particularly the evening news. In fact, many bright and decidedly sane people have chosen not to watch television news ever again. Period. Basically, the news (and TV is the worst) is a collection of the most horrible happenings in the world, condensed and served up to American families, daily, at six and ten. It is not realism. It is a formula for depression. It's no wonder our kids and teens are suffering from depression and apathy more than any other generation.

Your kids desperately need for you to affirm a future filled with bright, purposeful, joy-filled lives. Assume that they will do well, and convey that God has created them to accomplish marvelous things. Have fun wondering and dreaming with them what those things might be as they toddle, walk, and eventually fly from your parenting nest.

Her children arise and call her blessed.

PROVERBS 31:28

11

I Used to Have a Brain,
Then I Had Kids

Parents do a lot of gross things in the name of motherhood and fatherhood. It's doesn't matter on what economic level you live, when a child hands you a shoe with a knot in the shoestring that he has wet on all day long, the first thing you do instinctively is put it in your mouth and try to loosen up the knot with your teeth.

Erma Bombeck

Have you had a chance to read *My Little Bear*?" inquired my friend, Mindy, who had a degree in premed.

"No, I haven't," replied I, recipient of an alumni award at Texas A&M University. "Have you read *My Little Bunny*?"

What was happening to us? It was as if, with the birth of each child, we also lost a generous scoop of gray matter. Our hearts had long since convinced us to forego careers, if possible, in order to stay at home with our children, at least until they started school. But it wasn't always easy. I recall observing my husband studying the bestseller *Dress for Success* as he readied himself for a job interview and then taking a long gander at myself in a full-length mirror. Dressed in my faded purple Tweety Bird sweats, I felt qualified to write the "mom version" of the book *Dress Like a Mess.* (Subtitle: Because no matter how dressed for success you are, by the time your breasts have leaked twin circles of milk, the baby has spit up on your shoulder, and the toddler—covered in peanut butter and jelly—has hugged you right where his face hits your body, you are going to look more like an incontinent homeless person than a businesswoman anyway.)

So the question begs to be asked: "Why?" Why humble ourselves to the level of preschoolers? Why bend down to wipe the mouths (and worse) of a toddler when we could be bending the ear of executives, doctors, and grown-up audiences who (as a general rule) don't drool, whine, or bite?

Because our children gloriously light up our lives, even as they are messing up our living rooms, that's why.

It's the small things they say that enlarge our hearts. I remember taking my daughter, Rachel, at age three, to the bathroom at Burger King. From inside the bathroom stall I heard her little Southern accent. "I love you, Mommie. Aren't we both so sweet?"

Another day Zeke, our secondborn, took his grubby little hands and gently caressed mine as he said, ever so kindly, "Your hands are getting a little old, Mommy. But they're not as crumbly as Granny's." He was lost for a moment in his dreamy world, but then finished with, "I still love *her.*"

A glamorous career is nice, for sure. But moms the world

over who are loved unconditionally by their children will agree: There is nothing quite as gratifying, after all, as being sweet and crumbly.

Whoever loses his life for my sake will find it.

Matthew 10:39

12

Who's the Boss?

*What parent has not faced down the toddler
who declares through his outthrust bottom lip,
"You're not the boss of me!" Then ensues a
scene not unlike the shoot-out from High Noon.
Hopefully, Mom (or Dad) is the one left standing.*

BECKY FREEMAN JOHNSON

Everybody knows that children must be disciplined. That is, everyone except the children.

Being a soft touch, I knew I'd have a problem disciplining my children long before the day I discovered my firstborn, Zach, at age three, engrossed in the contents of my makeup kit. He loved to paint himself up like Geronimo or a clown. With proper anguish and indignation, I confiscated his supplies and began the scrub down.

Suddenly he pointed his chubby little finger at me and, in a voice that would have put Jeremiah and Isaiah in the shade, said, "I'm gonna tell God you took that makeup away from me!"

"Well," I responded firmly, "God sees everything, and He knows you got into my makeup without asking me."

Silence. Then very quietly he admitted, "Oh. I not be frazy about that."

I had to chuckle when a few days later, Zach walked up to me, my makeup kit in his outstretched hands, looking at it as a woman on a diet might gaze at a hot fudge sundae. Then very bravely he said, "You better take this away from me, Mom. I'm about to get into it."

I remember another near daily battle that would occur when Zach was around two. If I failed to cut his peanut butter sandwich into two perfect triangles, he would throw himself to the floor, thrashing and screaming as if in physical pain. I half-expected him to start foaming at the mouth. Needless to say, I either had to start the discipline process and get the kid under control or I'd need to purchase a tranquilizer gun. (Though I'm not sure if it would be for my toddler or me.)

Evidently, I had made an impact because a few weeks later when I made the fatal mistake of cutting Zach's sandwich diagonally from top left corner to bottom right, rather than vice versa, I was pleased with my son's maturing response. Instead of throwing his usual tantrum, he said with great restraint, "This is *not* funny, Mother."

No matter how successful we are at parenting, sooner or later comes a day when our children echo back to us words of discipline we have taught them. After a bedtime fiasco on an evening with no relief from a late-working, stressed-for-success daddy, I had come to the end of my patience. I ordered the boys to bed, plunked Rachel on the couch, and sentenced her to lie there until I could get a grip on myself. I began furiously loading the dishes into the dishwasher, grumbling to myself all the while until, like a balloon out of air, I exhausted my anger. Rachel, noticing a quieting in the kitchen, bravely peeked over the back of the couch. She smiled knowingly and spoke in a most maternal tone of voice.

"Are you ready to behave now?"

*No discipline seems pleasant at the time,
but painful. Later on, however, it produces
a harvest of righteousness and peace for
those who have been trained by it.*

Hebrews 12:11

13

Camper-to-Go!

*Life isn't measured by how many
breaths you take, but how many
moments take your breath away.*

Dr. Bob Moorehead

t was summertime in the piney woods of East Texas as I drove
our old station wagon through a set of iron gates (thankfully, they
were open) and cruised down a blacktop road. Just as I rounded a
curve I encountered a large animal. The beast had planted itself in
the middle of the road and there it stood, methodically chewing
its cud. Having grown accustomed to life outside the big city,
I wasn't all that shocked to come upon a hoofed, cud-chewing
animal sunning itself in the center of traffic. But this was a bovine

of a different color. This creature had a hump on its back, and its legs rose to the top of my station wagon. It was a camel—of the Arabian Desert variety.

The dromedary began eyeing my hood ornament hungrily and licking his chops in anticipation. Not knowing what to do, I honked the horn. All I got in response was the nonchalant blink of his ebony eyes. He would not be moved. What? Had I thought he could be honked into action like some common Hereford or Jersey?

Just then a long-legged cowboy strode by and tossed out some advice.

"I'd go around him if I was you. He's fixin' to spit."

And so I did. Speedily, in fact, and—may I add—none too soon. Welcome to Jan-Kay Ranch, Detroit, Texas.

I came to this unusual setting to bring Rachel and two of her girlfriends for a week of summer camp. Six-year-old Gabe tagged along for the ride. However, when he saw the camel, and then the llamas, antelopes, wild pigs, peacocks, and monkeys—and, of course, the tiger, bear, and baby elephant—it was all too much. How dare I bring him this close to Paradise, only to take him home again?

What is a good, sensible mother to do in such situations? I haven't the foggiest. I only know that this mother ended up leaving her son at camp with a plastic bag full of clothes scrounged from the recesses of her car.

I knew that if Gabe needed anything else, the family who owned the camp would fill in the gaps. After all, I'd gone to this very same ranch when I was a young girl. However, I decided to make a midweek visit, carrying with me fresh clothing rations for my little camper-to-go. Once I made it past the camel guard and parked my car—hood ornament intact—it didn't take long to locate Gabe. He was happily feeding Eedie the baby elephant fistfuls of popcorn. As I strolled up to say hello, I saw Eedie stretch out her trunk, grab the popcorn bag Gabe was holding, and, in an instant, gulp it down, paper and all.

Gabe was startled at first and then he got tickled as only little boys can—breaking out in a gale of spontaneous giggles. The scene of Gabe bent over with laughter and the elephant scarfing down his bag of popcorn went "click" in that place in my head where pictures I don't want to forget are stored.

Still, I worried that my youngest child may have experienced some homesickness, this being his first prolonged time away from home.

"So, Gabe," I asked gingerly, "have you had any crying spells? At night, maybe?"

"Yeah," he answered sheepishly. "Last night I did."

I nodded sympathetically and rubbed his back. He continued. "I cried because camp only lasts for three more days, and I want to stay forever."

He satisfies me with good things.

Psalm 103:5 NCV

14

Surprise Child

*If it looks like fun and it doesn't break
the Ten Commandments, do it.*

KAROL A. JACKOWSKI

My dear friend and neighbor of many years, Mary Sue, once asked, "Becky, have I ever told you about the first time I ever laid eyes on Gabe?" I wasn't quite sure I really wanted to hear this story, but she continued anyway.

"Well," she said, settling into a lawn chair, "I was taking a walk along the road, when suddenly this little boy pops out of nowhere from a nearby field, grabs my hand, and says, 'Come on!' Before I could even think, he led me down to the edge of the lake. Then he plopped down on his stomach by the bank and ducked his entire head underwater."

"That's my Gabe."

"That's not all. Then he lifted up his head, the water pouring in streams from his bangs, and hollered up at me, 'I learned how to duck my head under water today! Isn't that great?' "

How could she respond to such unbridled enthusiasm with anything but applause?

Gabe was my lastborn child. Number four on the heels of a very busy, mostly pregnant or nursing decade. I clearly remember the day that the dot on the pregnancy test turned blue. I did too. And yet, as any mother of a "surprise" child will tell you, they generally spend their life making up for the "pregnant AGAIN?" shock they caused you by sprinkling your life with sunshine from then on. They also tend to add spice to the lives of their older siblings, whether or not they wanted extra spice.

One morning when our secondborn, Zeke, was about 14 years old, he slunk in from the back door and gingerly made his way toward the kitchen. He was dripping wet and fully clothed. I raised my eyebrows in a silent question as Zeke shook his head and began to chuckle softly to himself. He weakly gathered up the hem of his soggy shirt and wrung some water into the kitchen sink in a futile effort to halt the puddling around him. Then he turned around and looked me full in the face, as if to be sure of my undivided attention. "Mom," he sighed, "you're not gonna believe what Gabe's done this time."

I handed Zeke a towel and leaned on the counter to take in the latest "crazy little brother" story. Zeke dabbed at his face and began. "I was sitting out on the dock this morning when I noticed something funny-looking out on the lake. It looked like maybe a duck caught in a trotline. So I jumped in and swam toward the bird to see if there was anything I could do to rescue the poor thing. When I got to it, however, my 'wounded duck' turned out to be nothing but a piece of Styrofoam with a pencil stuck in it."

I nodded, curious. Zeke continued. "There's more. On the pencil was a paper flag with a message on it in little kid handwriting. 'Hi. This is Gabe. I made this just for the fun of it.' "

Both of us simultaneously shook our heads, laughed, and said, "What are we going to do with that kid?" Of course we both knew what we'd do with him. What every family does with the funny, unique little lastborns among us.

We love them and savor the surprise "interruptions" and the color they continue to bring to our lives from the moment they turned our pregnancy test sticks bright blue.

*God...richly provides us with
everything for our enjoyment.*

1 TIMOTHY 6:17

15

Out of Sight, Out of Mind

I'm out of my mind; I'll be back in five minutes.

SEEN ON A BUMPER STICKER

Just for yuks, I recently purchased a bright orange key chain with the message, "Keys I Haven't Lost Yet" blazoned across the plastic tag. Then I drove to visit my eldest son, Zach, now in his early twenties, who was recovering from surgery in our local hospital. After staying several hours, I walked out of the hospital to my car, which was parked in the middle of the parking lot with no other cars around it at this late hour. And there, sticking out of the keyhole of the driver's side door, was the key chain swinging in the breeze. I couldn't help but wonder how many people walked by this scene that afternoon, doing double takes at the results of what had to be the most absentminded woman on the planet. I need a sticker to go with my keys to put on my forehead that says: "Brain I Haven't Lost Yet."

Needless to say, this default in my personality sometimes leaves my children more than a little jumpy. Zach was like a nervous cat every time I walked by his bed, twitching and bracing himself. Finally I asked him what he was so anxious about, and he said, "Mom, I'm scared to death you are going to get wrapped in my IV cord or my catheter and walk out with it attached to your purse." He didn't even grin when he said this. He just looked pained, as though he'd really, truly preferred that I stood about five feet away from him. At all times. I guess plastic tubing coming out of your body and a klutzy mother hovering nearby might do something to a kid's sense of humor.

I've been told by yet another child that I should do comedy for Alzheimer's patients and their families because of my uncanny ability to walk into a room and have no recall as to why I am there. My husband routinely finds normal things in odd places: a loaf of bread in the microwave, a jar of peanut butter in the garage, or a fork in one of his dress shoes. He no longer even asks why, or how, and certainly not who—he simply hands the misplaced items to me with a slow shake of his head, and I shrug my shoulders and grin. Honestly, there are many questions that I cannot answer, and it strains our collective logic to try.

One night I turned on the spigot to run water for my bath. Then I went downstairs. Soon I was distracted by the sight of dishes on the counter and decided I'd better do a little clean up. Suddenly—and to my great alarm!—I heard something that sounded like water running. *Now where in the world could that be coming from?* I mused. I called to my son Gabe, age 16 at the time, and, getting panicky at this point, told him I was afraid a pipe had burst. I announced with great concern that I could hear water pouring from somewhere; perhaps the washing machine line had a leak. No, the washing machine was fine. Together we frantically looked under the kitchen sink, and then we checked the hoses outside. Finally Gabe went upstairs, and then he plodded down them, slowly.

"Did you find the problem?" I asked, my eyes wide.

"Yes," he deadpanned. "I have the most forgetful mother in the world. Did you not remember you were running a bath upstairs?"

"Oh, yeah," I sheepishly admitted. "Oops."

Gabe pounded the palm of his hand against his head a few times, and then he did some deep breathing to calm himself.

Insanity is inherited. My kids swear they get it from their mother.

Comfort the feebleminded, support the weak, be patient toward all men.

1 THESSALONIANS 5:14 KJV

16

Like Mother, Like Daughter

Thank heaven for little girls.
SONG FROM *GIGI*

I loved my first two sons with all my heart. I'd even adjusted to snails, pails, and puppy dog tails. But a feminine soul by nature, I fervently prayed for a daughter with some sugar, spice, and everything nice. One who looked, walked, and talked like me. Someone who could speak fluent Girly-Girl.

About ten months later, my little Answer to Prayer made her grand entrance into the world. Perhaps when the Lord formed Rachel Praise He wanted to show me that each child is His own unique creation. Or perhaps God knew that the men in our family couldn't handle more than one talkative brunette.

Whatever His reasoning, Rachel came to us with wisps of soft blond hair and an amazingly quiet spirit.

May I explain that I'm not talking about the regular quiet type of "quiet"? I'm talking about a semi-comatose brand of "quiet." From the time our little girl was old enough to be aware of people, she developed an uncanny knack for "playing possum." Whenever someone would come over to coo over her and admire her, she'd focus her eyes straight ahead, look completely vacant, and her body would turn to stone.

The frustrating part of all this was that when Rachel was alone with me and her brothers she would transform before our very eyes into an animated, gurgling baby. This pattern continued until she was three and a half years old. She could talk my ears off as soon as a room was in an adult-free zone, but she stopped immediately when a grown-up wandered back into her space—it was like a game of freeze tag! With adults other than myself and her grandmothers, she managed to communicate by shaking her head up and down or back and forth, hoping they could understand through her brown eyes what she was inexplicably afraid to say with her mouth. It appeared to the entire world, with the exception of the aforementioned privileged few, that Rachel was hearing impaired. I couldn't believe it. How could any child of mine not want to be the life of the party?

There were some benefits to Rachel's quiet nature. For one, she was extremely affectionate—and portable. I could take her to any meeting and rest assured she would never utter a peep.

As Rachel passed from two to three-going-on-four, she especially adored her daddy, and the feeling was completely mutual. We knew this—not because she told him so or ever actually spoke—but she freely offered hugs, kisses, and lap-holding privileges to him. It was her father's nightly routine to rock her to sleep every night. They spoke not a word but were completely content with their silent cuddling ritual. Eventually, however, her dad began to long to hear the sound of his daughter's voice directed at him. For several weeks we tried everything we could think of without success, until finally the day came when we experienced the Big Breakthrough.

On this particular evening, her father gathered up Rachel in his arms along with her favorite storybook and retired with her to the couch in the living room where they could be alone. His plan was to read her book and purposely mispronounce and leave out some words. We knew how Rachel hated to leave any wrong unrighted. (She still hates it!)

Later he told the "rest of the story."

"Well, it was pretty slick. I started to read and I left out some words here and mixed up others there. Rachel was in agony, shaking her head 'no' so hard her blond hair was flying. I just kept right on reading. Pretty soon she put her face directly in front of mine and shook her head back and forth until I thought it might spin off her little neck. Finally, she could take it no more. 'Daddy!' she blurted. 'It not Berry the Moose. It Vera the Mouse!' Sweetest words I ever heard."

Slowly but surely Rachel continued to come out of her shell. By the time first grade arrived, she went unprotesting to school, and to our great relief, soon began to speak when called upon by her teachers.

Year by year I saw my shy little girl turn into a competent young woman.

In her senior year, Rach had to give a speech to 800 students at a student council rally in Austin. I feared for her as soon as I heard the news. Though she'd come a long way out of her shell, a first public speech to a crowd of 800 would make anyone's knees weak. I braced myself to help her through panic attacks. To my shock, she was as calm as a summer breeze about the whole thing. "After all," she told me before she left for the trip, "I've seen you do this sort of thing most of my life. If you can speak in public, I'm sure I can."

My mouth dropped open as I remembered the horrible fear I had to face in order to stand up in front of a crowd and not throw up on the front row. The hours, the money spent on seminars to help me overcome my fear of public speaking, the affirmations I memorized from *Feel the Fear and Do It Anyway.* My speech-making career was a hard-earned personal victory. And now my quiet child was waltzing to the podium as if she were born to it.

And, apparently, she was. She did BEAUTIFULLY.

By the time she turned 18 she was salutatorian of her high school class, and on her graduation day her family and classmates watched her give a lovely speech with such poise, grace, humor, and class that it took everything in me not to stand up, clap, and shout, "Bravo! Bravo!" All I could think in her moment of shining glory was, "Wow. She has grown up to be just like me."

(Of course, I later discovered that her father and grandparents were all thinking the very same thing. But this mother, without a doubt, knows best.)

Many daughters have done well,
but you excel them all.

PROVERBS 31:29 NKJV

17

Catch Her if You Can!

Never underestimate the speed of a toddler.

Becky Freeman Johnson

Though our daughter, Rachel, was a quiet, shy little girl, do not think for a moment this meant she was clingy and afraid of adventure. When she was just a few months old, we moved to our first place in the country, our nearest neighbors being a field away. Their two teenage daughters, Tracy and Dixie, loved to put Rachel in an open grain pail and carry her about by its handle when they went to feed their huge Charolais heifer, B.J.

When my baby girl reached the crawling age she often wore what I called "Sweet Pea" nightgowns. Zach and Zeke loved nothing more than to step on the hem of her sleeper, keeping her from actually covering any ground. She quickly learned to deliver the earsplitting squeal all brothers love to hear. They also taught her to stick out her tongue on command by saying, "Be a sassy girl, Rachel!" How ironic. She had the gall to stick out her tongue at strangers, but she couldn't bring herself to say the standard "bye-bye" or "patty-cake" for the benefit of an audience to save her life.

We soon learned that, though our little daughter was the silent type, she was faster than lightning. She had hurried herself into the world well in advance of the arrival of the midwife, and she had pretty much kept right on going. Being a fast little bugger and a remarkable climber, her quietness was actually dangerous at times. One cold spring morning when Rachel was about 18 months old, she and I enjoyed a bath together and I had just stepped out of the bathtub with her in my arms. I wrapped her in a towel and began to fluff her dry, but before I knew what had happened, she popped out of the towel like a banana out of its peel and shot out the bathroom door. I grabbed an old robe, donned it over my dripping self and ran after her in hot pursuit. By the time I reached the living room, the open front door told the tale.

I ran outside without my shoes, wet and freezing, and began to search the country landscape. As I tripped over rocks and crawled under barbed wire, I called out for my escaped toddler who was adorned this cold morning in nothing but her birthday suit. She was nowhere to be seen. My first thought was of Tracy and Dixie carting Rachel about their heifer's pen, and I felt a surge of anxiety. Surely not!

I raced to B.J.'s pen. No Rachel. I looked across the pasture and remembered the other, even larger black Angus bull—and real fear gripped me! As I ran through a field of stickers in my bare feet, I tripped and felt my big toe snap. Shaking off the pain and the blood, I hurried as fast as I could toward the bull and found him contentedly chewing his cud alone in the pasture. No sign of a naked baby, whole or flat.

Drained and near panic, I quickly hobbled toward Dixie and Tracy's house to see if their parents might be home to join me in my search for my diminutive streaker. When I reached their back porch, breathless and broken, I nearly tripped over the bare-skinned and sassy little toddler sitting on the steps. There was Rachel in all her glory, her tongue sticking straight out in my direction.

There's a saying here in Texas that men like their women a little on the sassy side. Rachel is now a fully grown woman, and her Texas beau tells me she's the perfect mixture of sweet 'n' sassy—when he can catch her! (It probably won't surprise you that Rachel ended up on the track team in high school and was an aerobics instructor in college.)

They will run and not grow weary,
they will walk and not be faint.

Isaiah 40:31

18

Angels to the Rescue

What do angels do?

They pull people out of burning cars and out of quicksand and keep people from being shot or falling out of airplanes, and help you with subtraction.

KIDS SAY THE GREATEST THINGS ABOUT GOD

As a child, and then as a mother, I always loved the song "Angels Watching Over Me." Scripture confirms that little ones have angels who are always looking at the face of the Father—and I believe they are looking at Him the way football players look at a coach. They are awaiting instructions for the next time they go out in the field to do battle on behalf of the home team, or in this case, a small child.

My cousin Jamie and her mother had taken Jamie's four young children along on a shopping trip to a mall in Houston. When they were pooped out, they stopped to rest a moment near the bottom of an escalator. As kids will do, little four-year-old Martha leaned her arms over the escalator's handrail, as she stood on the floor beside it watching people going up, up, up to the next level.

As the railing also rose, Martha lifted her feet off the ground for a ride and before anyone knew what was happening, her small body began rising above the mall floor. She was dangling only by her tiny arms to the escalator handrail. It all happened so fast that by the time Jamie looked up, screamed, and began sprinting up the steps to help her daughter, it was too late. When little Martha reached the top—20 feet above the ground—she also hit the wall. Her grandmother watched in helpless horror as she saw one little hand let go and then the other.

And that's when the angels took over. A woman standing below the escalator happened to see what was going on, positioned herself, said a silent prayer for strength, and opened her arms. As Martha fell toward the mall's tile floor, the woman made a successful catch. Both woman and child went down with the impact, but thankfully, both were unhurt. Of course, they were stunned.

Martha lay there in the woman's lap, perfectly still, not saying a word. Nothing seemed to be hurt, but she might have been in shock—or numb. After a long while, she wriggled and tugged at her rescuer's shirt. The woman leaned down closer to hear the quiet little voice. Amid the noise and turmoil and Jamie's crying and the grandmother's sighs of relief, Martha had one concern on her ladylike four-year-old mind.

"My unduhweauh is showing," she whispered.

The mother in me has to believe that somewhere, watching over a Houston mall, unseen to the naked eye, a couple of guardian angels gave each other a high five.

See that you do not look down on
one of these little ones. For I tell you
that their angels in heaven always see
the face of my Father in heaven.

MATTHEW 18:10

19

A Place of Grace

> *Joy tells me that once, years ago, she was haunted one morning by a feeling that God wanted something of her, a persistent pressure like the nag of a neglected duty and till mid-morning she kept on wondering what it was. But the moment she stopped worrying, the answer came through as plain as a spoken voice. It was, "I don't want you to do anything. I want to give you something" and immediately her heart was full of peace and delight.*
>
> C.S. Lewis

I was washing dishes at the kitchen sink several years ago when suddenly I heard something hit glass. Whirling around, I saw a tiny round hole in our living room window and then watched in disbelief as the huge 8′ x 4′ window cracked into a thousand pieces. Through this odd mosaic of glass, I saw that Gabe, about age seven at the time, had fallen to the ground outside.

I rushed out the door, but before I could reach him, he stood up, stared at the window in shock, threw his BB gun down on the ground, and ran around the house holding his hands over his eyes—as if by doing so he could shut out what had happened. I found him several minutes later on his big brother's bed, his head tucked under the covers, convulsed in tears.

"Gabe, Gabe," I said soothingly as I sat down near the lump on the bed, "it's going to be okay. Are you all right?"

"No!" he shouted, never one to stuff his feelings. Between sobs and from under the covers he cried, "I tripped and the gun fired up instead of down. I want to be invisible! I want to be in another country. I don't know what to do. I can't face Daddy! He just finished building that pretty room! Will you take me somewhere far away? I can live somewhere else!"

"Oh, Gabe," I said, holding his blanketed mummified form and rubbing what I guessed to be his back. "Accidents happen. All of us blow it sometimes. Think of all the stupid things I did this week. Remember how I left that important book out in the rain? And just last week, your daddy slammed into the front door with his back trying to move in a piece of equipment, and he shattered the glass in it. Daddy won't be upset—he knows how bad you feel already. I'll go get him and explain what happened. You'll see what I mean."

I left to find Scott and plead Gabe's case. I quickly informed him of the mishap and within minutes Gabe's father had taken my place as comforter there on the bed beside his grieving son. As I passed by the bedroom I saw father holding son in his arms, stroking his dark hair, telling stories of all the baseballs he'd thrown through windows when he was a kid.

"Son, it's just something little boys do at least once in their lives. You'll be more careful from now on. We're just glad you aren't hurt. Glass can be replaced; people can't." Gabe fell asleep within minutes, totally exhausted from his ordeal of self-flagellation.

Observing Gabe's trauma, I wondered, *Have I really changed all that much since I was a child? Aren't I more like a seven-year-old than I want to admit when it comes to making mistakes—punishing myself mentally over and over again for not being perfect?* And all along, my Father is there beside me, holding out comfort, and saying, "Becky, did you forget again? You don't have to be perfect. You don't even have to be all that good at anything. Just be yourself. I forgave you long ago, so forgive yourself—and let Me rock you and hold you and love you when you blow it. Then get back up and go after it again. I'll be here whenever you need Me."

Charles Spurgeon, who battled depression and low moods, once said, "The strong are not always vigorous, the wise not always ready, the brave not always courageous, and the joyous not always happy." We can't let our mistakes or temporary downtimes or even our lapses into sin define who we really are. We may be acting weak, depressed, and immature. Who we are is what God sees. Because what God sees, when He looks at our hearts, is Jesus.

There is no fear in love. But perfect love drives out fear, because fear has to do with punishment.

1 JOHN 4:18

20

I Don't Care How Big and Famous You Are. I'm STILL Your MOTHER!

They sit on our shoulders and whisper in our ears, even when they're a thousand miles away.
BECKY FREEMAN JOHNSON AND RUTHIE ARNOLD

As I write this, the Super Bowl is about to start in the living room. I know nothing about it. In fact I just hollered in the general direction of the guys gathered around the TV and asked, "Who is playing and who am I supposed to root for?"

Gabe said I should cheer for the Raiders because there are a lot of old guys on that team and I am an old woman. Excuse me while I go bop my son with a pillow.

There. I feel better now. No matter how old our children

get, or how wisecracking they become, they are still our little boys and girls. This is why, at the end of the big game today, the camera will zoom in on huge sweaty men in football uniforms who will be reduced to little boys as they grin into the lens and say, "Hi, Mom!"

It's our job to make sure that there is one place in the world where a grown man can always come home and get a hug, a cookie, and a little lecture. We know about modern day moms who rocked the babies that are rocking our world: Michael Jordan's mother, George W. Bush's mom…but what about other great mothers?

Some astute mother sent me the following quotes from the great unsung mothers in our history:

PAUL REVERE'S MOTHER: "I don't care where you think you have to go, young man. Midnight is past your curfew."

MONA LISA'S MOTHER: "After all that money your father and I spent on braces, that's the biggest smile you can give us?"

COLUMBUS'S MOTHER: "I don't care what you've discovered. You still could have written!"

MICHELANGELO'S MOTHER: "Can't you paint on walls like other children? Do you have any idea how hard it is to get that stuff off the ceiling?"

NAPOLEON'S MOTHER: "All right, if you aren't hiding your report card inside your jacket, take your hand out of there and show me."

ABRAHAM LINCOLN'S MOTHER: "Again with the stovepipe hat? Can't you just wear a baseball cap like the other kids?"

MARY'S MOTHER: "I'm not upset that your lamb followed

you to school, but I would like to know how he got a better grade than you."

ALBERT EINSTEIN'S MOTHER: "But it's your senior picture. Can't you do something about your hair? Styling gel, mousse, something?"

GEORGE WASHINGTON'S MOTHER: "The next time I catch you throwing money across the Potomac, you can kiss your allowance goodbye!"

JONAH'S MOTHER: "That's a nice story. Now tell me where you've really been for the last three days."

THOMAS EDISON'S MOTHER: "Of course I'm proud that you invented the electric lightbulb. Now turn it off and get to bed."

(Source unknown, Internet)

You can lead a CEO of a large corporation to water, but if he's in his childhood home he can't drink it without his mother telling him to wash the cup, put it up, and wipe his mouth.

We all need someone to keep us humble. This is why God gave us mothers.

Speaking the truth in love, we are to grow up.

Ephesians 4:15 nasb

21

Miraculous Mud

What does God do?

*God makes bees with little wings
all day. Probably out of mud.*

KIDS SAY THE GREATEST THINGS ABOUT GOD

Mud.

Okay, Moms. What does that word bring to mind? A messy kitchen floor? Scraping dried mud mixed with grass off of small tennis shoes? (I've always thought the government should look into building bombproof shelters from the gunk that dries on kids' shoes.)

Sometimes it helps to take the same word, shrink yourself mentally to the size of a small child, and try it again. Become a little six-year-old girl in your mind's eye for just a moment. Now what do you think of when I say the word "mud"?

Mud...glorious mud. Remember the squish-squashy feel of it oozing up between your toes? Or becoming a backyard pastry chef—decorating mud pies with chocolate dirt and candy rocks and twig candles?

Raising our family on a lake was always a bit fun, but when the lake was drained one summer, our backyard became the place for high adventure. Although my kids had to forego a summer of fishing and waterskiing, they had—muddin'. "What's muddin'?" you ask. Perhaps I should simply explain how muddin' is carried out, and I think you'll get the general idea.

To get the most from the muddin' experience, you first pull on the tallest pair of rubber boots you can find—hip boots are best. Then, starting from the shore, the object of the game is to wade toward the middle of what used to be the lake, venturing out and in as deep as you dare. Our teenagers routinely made it clear up to their necks in black goop. And that's about the gist of it.

"Why would anyone in his or her right mind want to do this?" you may ask. I don't know. Believe me, I don't know. I was a child of more dainty constitution, myself. But my kids absolutely loved this activity, and since it kept them busy and happy, I held my tongue. As long as they sprayed off with the hose in the yard before setting a toe on the carpet, I was pretty easygoing about such things.

I inherited this attitude, I think, from my own mother. She never blinked about letting us kids play outside in the rain. In reference to such leniencies (or lunacies, as the case may be), one of my boys once complimented me by saying, "Mom, I'm so glad you aren't sensible like other kids' moms."

Perhaps being a sensible mother is overrated. When you look back at your own childhood, do you think warm thoughts about the times your mother was sensible? When most of us search our memories for the warmest, happiest scenes from childhood involving our moms, we pull up times when they broke the mold, when they were most UN-sensible. The time she grabbed you in the hall and tickled you to the floor. The time she let you make a fort in the living room. When she gave you a bowl of pink frosting and let you have a go at painting a batch of cookies (and the counter and the table and the front of your shirt and the floor…) with gusto. Or when she playfully sprayed you with the water hose as you walked by her watering the lawn.

The next time it starts to rain outside and you start to go on automatic Sensible Mom pilot and start to call the kids inside so they won't get wet—pause, instead. Think like a Fun Mom. Perhaps you'll end up joining them for a dance in the rain.

And give them a warm memory to mull over when they are your ripe old age.

Your mother was like a vine in your vineyard planted by the water; it was fruitful and full of branches because of abundant water.

EZEKIEL 19:10

22

Never Too Late for Second Childhood

Blessed is he who keeps his child-heart alive.

AUTHOR UNKNOWN

I was in California speaking when the event planner handed me a surprise: two tickets to Disneyland. I was less than overjoyed. Actually, I'd planned on reading by the pool, napping in the hotel room, and heading home. Something a little more grown-uppy.

I kindly explained the situation. "I'm just here with a friend of mine. We don't have our kids with us."

"Oh," she said with a grin and wink as she handed me the tickets. "You'll REALLY have fun, then!"

And that's how I ended up walking through the gates of Disney's Magic Kingdom as an exhausted adult and coming back out that same entrance, several hours later, as an exuberant child.

My friend Melissa and I flew above London's rooftops on our way to Neverland. We sat entranced at the intricate detail and diversity of the famous "It's a Small World" ride. (Though I believe if I had to hear the chorus of that repetitive song one more time I might go out of my small, small mind.) I wondered, perplexed, at the new virtual reality rides. *I mean, how do they DO that? How do they make you feel as though you've just sped through galaxies in a starship?*

But my favorite part of all was the parade. Not just any parade. The Lion King Parade. Disney style. Never in all my life have I seen such a gorgeous display, such beautiful music, right where I could reach out and touch it. I found myself—in spite of the grown-up within—caught up in the fantastic display as dancers of all nationalities in brilliant costumes ascended poles and floats and swayed to the beautiful rhythms of the song "The Circle of Life."

By evening the transformation was complete. I was a grinning fool, sporting a Mickey Mouse shirt and a matching beanie complete with propeller.

"Melissa," I said to my friend as we stopped for a rest and a bite to eat, "look at me! Can you believe I've bought into the whole commercialized deal—Cap'n Hook, line and sinker?"

"I noticed," said Melissa, aiming a camera in my mouse-eared direction. "It happens to the best of us. Face it, Becky. You've been Disneyed."

We found a table near a jazz band and dance floor and propped our weary feet on a nearby chair. The band started up, playing the romantic, toe-tapping music of the 1940s era. Melissa and I visited with some teenagers during the break who were elegantly dressed in '40s regalia. They'd been having a ball, swing-stepping together under the stars, a new trend among teens. (They told us they come out several times a week just for some good, wholesome fun. I know. Could have knocked us over with a feather too.)

The breeze was soft around my face. The gentle caress gave me a twinge of homesickness. I wished—okay, yes, "upon a star"—that my husband could have been there with me at that moment. He'd have had me out on that dance floor in no time. And we'd have given those young whippersnappers a run for their money.

From the corner of my eye I could see a young father buying his little boy some ice cream. The child reached up for the cone, his chubby hand eager for the cold, dripping sweetness. Then the band, in the background, began playing what is, perhaps, my favorite song. Slow and sweet, its melody melted the simple smile of the evening into my memory. For I believe Louis Armstrong captured for all time the essence of childlike joy when he flashed his famous grin and gifted us with "What a Wonderful World."

As the last strains of the music wound down, the little boy finished off his last bite of ice cream. Then just as the raspy-voiced crooner sang the final, "What-a-won-der-ful-world," the child—as if on cue—clapped his sticky hands together, grinned for all he was worth, looked straight at me and shouted, "Yeah!"

I looked at him and shouted, "Yeah!" right back at him.

And for that enchanted moment, connecting on some kind of kid frequency, the world indeed seemed sparkling and amazing and completely wonderful.

Which is why we moms need to take time away from our children now and then to simply experience being childlike again, as if for the very first time.

Yeah?

Oh, yeah.

They will still bear fruit in old age,
they will stay fresh and green.

PSALM 92:14

23

The Frog and I

It is children—tender of heart and low to the earth—who are the connoisseurs of creation.

BECKY FREEMAN JOHNSON

Even at age nine, Gabe was as critter-loving a kid as I've ever seen. On his desk during that third grade year, I counted two turtles, one frog, two hermit crabs, and about a dozen tadpoles swimming in—what else?—my best crystal bowl. I put up with a lot when it comes to matters of the heart. And for Gabe, frogs and turtles and tadpoles and such are definitely affairs of the heart.

Once, just once, in an effort to be "cool," Gabe broke his own little frog-loving heart. And I'll never forget it.

That fateful afternoon Gabe burst into the house and dived

onto my bed, wrapping a sheet tightly around his head. Being the sensitive and observant mother that I am, I sensed right away something might be amiss.

"Gabriel," I coaxed, "what's the matter, honey?"

Nothing. No response from under the covers.

"Gabe, you can tell me *anything*. Have you done something wrong?"

There was a slight movement in the affirmative from the mummified form.

"Well, there's nothing you've done that can't be forgiven. Come on out and let's talk."

When he finally unraveled himself from the sheets I was taken aback by the flood of tears on his face and the obvious agony of soul in his eyes.

"What, honey, what?" I asked softly, shaking my head and searching his face for clues.

After a few gulps he finally managed to say, "I…gigged…a…frog."

"Oh, dear," I said, remembering that Gabe's big brothers had been into gigging bullfrogs for sport and then cooking their game's legs for meat. I'd never approved of it, but I know boys will be boys and tried not to think about the "frog hunting" going on in nearby ponds.

And now it was clear. Gabe, trying to be a big hunter like his brothers, had taken a kitchen fork and "gigged" a small frog, thinking he'd bring home frog leg "game" like the big guys.

"Oh, Gabriel," I said, swallowing a lump in my throat, "did it surprise you when you realized you had hurt something you've always loved?"

"Mo-o-mmm," he sobbed into my shoulder, his small fingers

squeezing tightly into my arms, "I didn't think about it hurting him until it was over!"

I found myself swallowing lumps in my own throat all the while I was trying to convince my son he could be forgiven for his mistake.

"I'm so sorry! I didn't mean to do such a sad, sad thing. I didn't know it would hurt you this bad!"

In truth, I wasn't stifling tears for Gabe's heinous crime. It was because I identified with him so much. Have we not all, at one time or another, hurt something we loved and held dear? Haven't I "gigged" the ones I love the most with careless or hateful words? And then suffered the weight of my guilt, wishing—oh, wishing so hard—that I could turn back the clock and erase something awful I'd said or done? Every child, every man, and every woman has at one time or another come face-to-face with the fact that they've just gigged an innocent frog.

That is, if they are still tenderhearted enough to admit it. We so easily become calloused, but tenderheartedness is one of the most precious childlike qualities God asks us to cherish on into adulthood. But I digress. Back to the Frog Tragedy before us.

What's a mother to do in the face of such angst and repentance?

Dry the tears. Have a proper burial. (Where, in desperation to comfort my son, I stretched all theological lines by making up incredible stories about green clouds and froggie heaven.)

Then we go back to loving frogs—this time with a deeper awareness of how precious and dear and inescapably beautiful are all the things that have been created by God's hand.

A few months after the frog-gigging crisis, Gabe and I were walking hand in hand along our country road. Out from the woods a box turtle lumbered into view. Gabe looked up at me and then grinned toward heaven.

"Oh, wow, Mom," he said reverently. "That's TWO."

"Two what?" I asked, peering down at his upturned face.

"That's two turtles in one day! Man, God sure has been good to me."

(From this anecdote emerged a family saying. Any really great day, one of double blessings, is now and forever known as a Two-Turtle Day.)

With the sighting of those turtles, Gabe knew, as only a child can know, that all had been forgiven—for God smiles on the kind and tenderhearted, even though we sometimes blow it big time.

Be gentle and ready to forgive; never hold grudges. Remember, the Lord forgave you.

Colossians 3:13 TLB

24

Kids Brake for Rainbows

*Hold every moment sacred. Give each clarity
and meaning, each the weight of thine
awareness, each its true and due fulfillment.*

THOMAS MANN

Are you familiar with a famous Tim Conway skit? The one in which he plays an old man with Einstein hair who shuffles along at the speed of a wounded snail? The skit varies in theme, but the outcome is always the same—he drives his fellow actors insane, their nerves worn to the nubs by the old man's earnest, but barely perceptible, efforts at moving or doctoring or repairing.

Well, I ran into the Cracker Barrel yesterday to get a few Christmas presents and on the way out the door found myself ground to a near halt by a herd of Mr. and Mrs. Scoot-Along

Conways enjoying an outing with their senior adult Sunday school class. Though I love elderly people, I was in a big hurry and found my forbearance in short supply. By the time the group had inched their way from the front door down the steps to the parking lot, I had overheard which Beanie Babies were purchased for assorted grandchildren, what each member had especially enjoyed for lunch, and the effect of such a lunch on a bevy of internal organs. (All this accompanied by hand motions and special sound effects.)

I finally found an escape hatch through the gang of shuffling seniors, and as I made a sneak break for my car, it dawned on me that it had been a long time since I'd been forced to move at such a slothlike pace. The last time, in fact, that I'd been put in slow motion confinement was when I took my last toddler on a trip to the mall.

Just getting the toddler from car to stroller to inside the mall was like trying to herd cats. In my years as a mother of four preschoolers, I've lost track of how many times I found myself moving in zombielike fashion through the mall toy store, a toddler leading me from Ugly Toy to Useless Toy in an "I Want Dat!" frenzy. The stroller was soon reduced to a decorative trailer for hauling the diaper bag, and I was reduced to a decorative appendage being hauled by the toddler, who long ago decided to take control of the situation.

Once, desperate for a break, I stopped at the food court to buy chicken nuggets to share between the baby and me. (Nourishment for the slow death march back to the car.) But soon I discovered my child was already snacking on an appetizer of roach body parts, his tiny fingers having deftly pried them up from a crack in the table while I turned for the half second it took to open the dipping sauce. I offered him a sip of milk, hoping to dilute the bug toxins, which he spit across the table, spraying the back of the mall janitor's head—his cute little way of saying, "I wanted root beer!"

The best thing about having to take small children on errands for several years in a row is that you will forever after be grateful for life's small, speedier blessings. Oh, the bliss of simply grabbing your keys, a lightweight purse, and zipping around town again. No buckles, no bags, no strollers to cramp your style or bog down your step. Like the little lisping, impassioned mouse from *An American Tail,* you feel like shouting, "Fweedom! Fweedom!" You are released from ever having to drag down endless rows of plastic toys. You may choose to never eat a preformed, lukewarm trapezoid of chicken again.

It occurs to me that we slowly toddle our way into the world, then somewhere along the way we pick up speed until we reach midlife and find ourselves practically racing through our days. Then, a few years later, when we are able to spy the "Exit Life" sign on the horizon, we put the brakes on and began easin' up on the gas. We Sunday drive as slowly as possible on our way out of this world. As Harold Munro said, "Here's a new day. O Pendulum, move slowly!"

"What's the hurry?" both toddlers and the elderly—stationed at each end of life's poles—seem to ask. "You might miss something interesting if you go too fast. Might pass up a cricket head or a rainbow shimmering off an oil spot. Or a nice pea salad."

The only difference is that the elderly admonish us to "stop and smell the roses," while toddlers simply eat them.

Be still, and know that I am God.

Psalm 46:10

25

Bubbles from Heaven

*The most wasted of all our days are those
in which we have not laughed.*

Nocholas-Sebastian Chamfort

One day I was driving along our country road with Gabriel in the front seat. In front of us was a car, and in front of the car was a pickup truck. (Of course, in Texas you are never more than a car's length from a pickup.) In the back of the truck was a large bag of groceries that suddenly fell to the road. In that sack was an industrial-sized bottle of blue-green shampoo. I know this because the car ahead of us had run over the shampoo and its contents were now on my windshield. I could not see a thing.

I glanced at Gabe, whose eyebrows had disappeared under

his bangs, so astonished was he. Not knowing what else to do, I flipped on the windshield wipers, which only succeeded in spreading the blue-green mess in a nice EVEN layer across the windshield. *What to do now?* I thought as I peered through the driver's side window in an effort to see the road in front of me.

Just at that moment, as if on cue, a summer rain began to fall. The shampoo turned into a sort of lovely moving bubble bath, with soap bubbles now lifting and floating from our car and into the air.

We pulled up into our driveway at home and I put the car into "park." The rain stopped, the sun came out, and my windshield was sparkling clean. Once again I looked over at Gabe. His face was frozen in the eyebrows-lifted position. Finally he found his voice.

"Mo-o-o-m," he began tentatively, "do other kids' moms have this kind of stuff happen to them?"

I knew what he was thinking. I knew he was thinking that God had decided it was time to personally wash his mother's dirty windshield because she was just never going to get around to it.

All I could do was smile and say, "Well, son, I can't really say if other kids' moms have this stuff happen to them as often as odd things seem to happen to me. It's a bit of a mystery. But I do think God likes to surprise people who don't mind being surprised."

Then I rolled down my window and stuck my head out. "Thank you for the sunshine!" I said into the heavens. "And for the clean windshield!"

And I imagined a celestial smile beaming in our direction.

Do you think the God of the universe takes time to touch your heart or feather-tickle your funny bone? Is it crazy to think that the Lord enjoys sharing a good laugh with us as much as we love chuckling over a funny incident with a good friend?

I don't think so. Quaker theologian Elton Trueblood wrote a classic book called *The Humor of Christ,* pointing to the importance of visualizing our Savior's smile and inherent wit. So be on the lookout for God's smile at you.

And watch out, as well, for projectile shampoo.

*May the Lord's face radiate
with joy because of you.*

Numbers 6:25 tlb

26

Theology of the Sparrow

___

I sing because I'm happy,
I sing because I'm free!
His eye is on the sparrow,
And I know He watches me.

"HIS EYE IS ON THE SPARROW"
CIVILLA D. MARTIN

I owe the crux of my theological position on suffering to Jill Briscoe. I am from the South, and people tell me that everything I say sounds more humorous with my Texas twang behind it. Jill is English, and to me, everything she says sounds slightly more brilliant and profound because of her lovely British accent.

One evening before I stood to speak, Jill went before me and shared some lessons from Scripture. Time has erased the memory of most of what she said, I confess, but one thought entered my head with such profundity, it sank into my heart and took residence there.

"God never said a sparrow wouldn't fall to the ground," she said with loving compassion to an auditorium full of women. "He only promised to be with the sparrow if and when he fell."

And with those words I settled a long-standing issue. God never promised us an easy, pain-free life. Author Donna Partow penned a title to her book that says so well how many of us feel at midlife: *This Isn't the Life I Signed Up For.*

What, then, can we cling to if at any moment our lives could change? (Or if at any moment our human nature could cause our own fall to the ground of despair?)

Christ Himself.

We are not guaranteed anything in this life except for one thing: His presence.

The gift that suffering brings to us is the realization that He is truly enough. And when it doesn't feel that He is enough, He usually sends one of His children to be His vessel of love, comfort, and encouragement. Then, working through people, we see God.

For often, the love you see in someone's eyes as you walk through pain is a glimpse of God Himself. As the lyrics of a beautiful song from *Les Miserables* asserts, "To love another is to see the face of God."

Shortly after the world was stunned by the events of September 11, 2001, my own world fell apart in one 9-1-1 crisis after another. In the summer of 2002, I found myself sitting in a therapist's office, soaking tissue after tissue with my tears. His name was Wil, and he too had lived through the same sort of pain I was trying to accept and survive: the loss of a long-term marriage. But he was further down the road to recovery. He'd had five years to adjust and find his smile again. I was still in shock, and so fragile I feared I might break.

"How did you do it? Where did you find the peace you enjoy today?"

"Becky," he said, leaning back in his chair and catching my eyes with his in a benevolent gaze. "Do you remember when Jesus said that when He went away, He would send another Comforter, and when He came that we would receive a joy that no man could take away?"

I nodded, dabbing at my eyes.

"Well, when we suffer great loss, and survive with God's help, we receive something precious. We experience a joy in spite of loss, a joy that no thing and no person can ever take away from us. This is no small gift, Becky, to know the nearness of God's love no matter your circumstances."

Sometimes I forget this truth. I cling to circumstances or people who I believe will fulfill me and give me joy. But the truth is, God produces the joy from within. Happiness is an inside job. And because it comes from Him, from the well of His Spirit within, we do not have to be dependent on anything or anyone to experience the joy no man can take away.

The gift of Himself, His presence, is enough.

Surely I am with you always.

MATTHEW 28:20

27

Love Him Tender, Lord

"Tell me, are you a Christian, child?"
"And I said, 'Ma'am, I am tonight.'"
FROM "WALKING IN MEMPHIS"

My youngest son has had a longtime fascination with everything Elvis: music, movies, biographies, anecdotes, looks. You name it. In fact, Gabriel is a near Elvis look-alike with smoky dark eyes, a smile that could melt butter, and a sweet Southern-suave way of acting around girls (who almost audibly swoon when he walks into a room).

Elvis isn't dead. In fact, for many years he lived in my house: upstairs, down the hall, two doors to the left.

But my little Elvis Junior suffered one of the hardest years of his life as a teen. He was the last kid living at home when our 27-year marriage came apart at the seams. He and his young girlfriend of four years broke up. Within a year of each other, two of his good friends were killed too young—one in a car accident (Justin was my daughter-in-law Amy's little brother) and another in a drowning, just two doors down from us, in our beloved backyard lake (Josh was my best friend Melissa's son).

Gabe, as so many boys of divorce, found himself in the role of comforter to his mom, and sometimes to his dad as well. He was strong for Zeke and Amy. He was strong for Melissa (who was like Gabe's second mother). He was strong for his girlfriend, Allison, whose parents also divorced at the same time.

He was just 15-going-on-16 when so many lives fell apart around his broad shoulders. Shoulders that too often seemed to hold the weight of the world on them.

One day Gabe came into my bedroom and lay across the bed. He'd had a good hard cry, one that had been pent up for who knows how long. After the cleansing relief that tears bring, he looked at me soulfully and said, "Mom, I don't think I have had a stress-free week in two years."

I wanted to scoop him up in my lap, the way I did when he was three, and kiss away all the boo-boos of pain he'd had to deal with at such a tender age.

"What things can you do for yourself that help you to feel better?" I asked. And he said that for some reason Elvis songs always put him in a better mood. (I find that Sinatra's snappy tunes lift my spirits. I know, perhaps, that I should reach for a CD of hymns, or at least Australian praise songs. But I have to admit that when it comes to curing a bad case of the blues around our house, we break for Elvis or Sinatra.)

At this point our family had been through plenty of soul-searching and therapy, examining what went wrong. We were well acquainted with grief. But there comes a moment when it is time to slow down the crying and crank up the living again. Exit the Garden of Gethsemane and enter the Garden of the Resurrection. In my heart I knew that Gabe needed to get a fresh glimpse of the world and to have some good old-fashioned fun.

I checked my speaking calendar and noted that I had an engagement in Tennessee, right between Memphis and Nashville. With a couple of phone calls it was all arranged. Gabe and I were goin' to Graceland.

In a small town near Memphis, Gabe heard me speak to an audience for the first time. He'd been avoiding it all these years, secretly afraid that his mother might turn into one of those "fake TV preachers" when given a microphone, stage, and podium. I'll never forget the look on his face as he watched me from the audience. He kept staring at me and then around at the women taking notes, who went from paying rapt attention to wiping their tears or doubling over with laughter. Later, standing at my book table, he absolutely ate up the Southern hospitality of the ladies and young teenage girls who asked for his autograph. (He was beyond stunned when a line formed for people wanting to buy some of his mother's books—books we were always tripping over and stepping around in some room of our house, books that had become almost a part of the furniture to my family throughout my writing years.)

After the event Gabe climbed in the passenger seat of our rental car, picked up the cell phone, and immediately dialed a friend. "You aren't goin' to believe this," he said incredulously. "I just heard my mom speak, and all she does is act the same way she does when she drives us home from school in the car—and these people love her, think she is hilarious, and pay her for it!"

Gabe's newfound awe lasted all of about 30 minutes before we'd settled back into our comfortable mom-and-son routine, with him scolding me about my terrible driving. But having his awe was nice while it lasted.

The next morning we hopped aboard a tour bus and made our way through Elvis's beloved Graceland as we sported headphones filled with the King of Rock 'n' Roll's music and narration. I could not help but notice how small this world-famous mansion seemed, and though some of the rooms were unique indeed, the kitchen could have been just about anyone's kitchen from the 1970s—simple, cozy, and functional. Though Elvis was (and is) a controversial figure, it was obvious he had a loving and generous heart—especially toward his mama, which pleased me. And though Gabe has struggled with a God who allowed so much up-close-and-personal-pain to hit our family and friends—he's drawn to Elvis's gospel songs and the rock 'n' roll icon's obvious hunger for God's love and peace in a heart that was often in turmoil.

The next morning was Sunday, and Gabe and I drove to the Elvis Restaurant on famous Beale Street in downtown Memphis. As we walked in, a casually dressed band was singing some of Presley's favorite gospel songs in his soulful style. Over pancakes and coffee and "How Great Thou Art" and "Amazing Grace," Gabe and I ate and listened, and at one point looked up, caught each other's eyes, and smiled. I could sense peace and relaxation on my son's face, and even some happiness. Some of the joyful little kid I remembered seemed to be returning to this melancholy teenager.

"We're healing, Gabe," I said. "We are all going to be okay.

You and I, your father, your brothers, and your sister are going to be *just fine.*"

He nodded and lifted his orange juice in acknowledgment.

"In fact," I continued, "the future is so bright I think we're going to need shades. Why don't you and I go next door and buy some?"

Within 20 minutes we were "walking in Memphis" with our feet ten feet off of Beale like two starstruck tourists, each sporting a pair of Elvis Presley embossed sunglasses.

The sun shone down on us as Gabe lowered his huge Hollywood silver shades, grinned, and said, "Thankyaverymuch, Mama. Thankyaverymuch."

Then we got in the car, and drove away—with Graceland in our rearview mirror, a CD of Elvis singing "Take My Hand, Precious Lord," and a significant corner having been turned in our lives.

Every good and perfect gift is from above, coming down from the Father of the heavenly lights, who does not change like shifting shadows.

JAMES 1:17

28

Gourmet Moments

*There are no great things, only
small things with great love.*
MOTHER TERESA

At this writing I am sitting on a back porch in Hot Springs,
Arkansas. It's an early summer evening; the air is pleasantly cool
and the sun is still warm on my shoulders. Off in the distance
lush green hills surround the sparkling lake in front of me like
giant maternal arms holding a basin of water.

We came here—me, Gabe, Melissa and her daughter, Sarah,
and two other teen friends—to relax at the end of a crisis-filled,
hectic school year. As soon as we arrived at our condo, I walked
outside to take a breath of fresh air and generally seek some quiet

in which to unwind. Just as I began to sink into a lawn chair, I heard a scream. I looked up and saw that the distress call was coming from the direction of the swimming pool.

So much for relaxation.

The yelp for help came from a young girl, about age 15, who was sitting on the edge of the pool, her legs dangling in the water. "What's the matter?" I hollered in her direction as I hurriedly walked toward the pool.

"I hurt my leg real bad!" she said between moans.

Once there I took a good look at her leg and at her anguished face—turning pale at this point—and guessed it was either broken or badly sprained. I instructed one of her friends to stay with her and another to find the girl's mom as I ran for pillows and a blanket. Upon my return to the scene of the crisis, another vacationing rescuer, a kind-faced man in his late fifties or early sixties, was also heading toward the pool with a blanket in hand.

I sat down by the girl, whose name, I learned, was Christine, and tucked a pillow under her head and another one under her hurt leg and rubbed her arm.

"I wish I were a nurse," I said compassionately, "but I'm just a mama, so I'll do the best I can to mother you until your mom or a paramedic arrives." She seemed grateful as I played Florence Nightingale—chatting while stroking her head and then patting her hand as I talked. At one point I looked up at the neighbor with the blanket and introduced myself. "Looks like we are the designated nurturers of Condoville."

He smiled, extended his hand, and said, "You have me pegged. My name is Tom. Pleased to meet you."

Before long we had a little caring crowd gathered. The mother, having just woken up from a nap, was trying to get oriented and confused about what to do next. So Tom and I—like temporary surrogate parents—consulted and decided it was better to be safe than sorry, and that an ambulance should be called to the scene of the pain. Christine was obviously in way too much discomfort to be moved.

By the time the paramedics arrived, I was so into my caretaker role that the attendants assumed I was Christine's mother. I laughed and said, "I am sorry. I'm not *her* mom. I am just a generic, empathetic mother-at-large."

As the paramedics took information from the real mother, I looked down at Christine and said, "Honey, how did you do this?"

She winced and said, "Well, my friend saw some boys come out of a condo and said, 'Hey, look at those cute guys!' and I turned to look and somehow got my foot twisted up in the swimming pool ladder."

I looked around and said, "Were the boys, by any chance, the ones who are walking by the lake right now?"

"Uh-huh," she said pitifully. "That's them."

"Oh, dear," I said with a smile, "one of those boys is my son Gabe. He has broken a few hearts, but I think this may be the first time he caused a broken leg."

The next morning Tom was at the door. Soon the news of Christine's condition had circulated through our little resort neighborhood. She had a severe break across the femur and had to have surgery in order to set the bone. We delivered our get well wishes to the family.

Last night Tom and his wife, Judy, asked Melissa and me out for a delicious Italian meal. The restaurant they chose was up on a hill overlooking a lake. Tom had prearranged everything so that when we arrived the maître d' seated us and brought plate after plate of fine food.

Touched by his gesture of kindness, I said, "Tom, this reminds me of the movie *Babette's Feast,* where a woman spends every dime she has to create an unforgettable dinner for her friends. You are giving us this lovely evening, and we've done nothing to deserve it."

Tom smiled and confessed that he had spent several years in Paris. "It was there that I learned to slow down and savor a good meal and good friends. I remember watching a Frenchwoman slowly cut a simple orange and arrange it so beautifully that it was like a piece of art. I'll never forget that orange. It symbolized to me the importance of noticing small things, small moments, and making the most of them."

"You have a good heart," I said to him, and as I looked in his eyes, I saw a bit of Jesus reflected there.

"You do too," he said.

"How do you know that?"

"You brought a blanket."

"So did you."

With that, he held out his arms and we all joined hands as Tom offered a prayer of thanksgiving for food, friendship, and caring. In that moment I realized that tending to another human being in the simplest of ways—to extend a kindness just because you can—is one of the greatest joys of life, infusing the mundane with meaning.

When you bring someone a blanket, when you calm a furrowed brow, when you create a luscious dinner or peel an orange with love—you are joining Christ in bringing a bit of warmth and light to a world that is cold, lonely, and hungry.

Do not despair, Mom, as you watch your chicks fly from your nest. For once a mama, always a mama, and this world needs all the mothers it can hold. Even if your children are all grown-up, God uses semi-retired mothers in small, magnificently simple ways to bring sunshine to His children.

I tell you the truth, anyone who gives you a cup of water in my name...will certainly not lose his reward.

MARK 9:41

From Becky Freeman Johnson...

○ ○ ○

With my new marriage and a nearby (and ever-growing) passel of children-turned-adults, I've taken on lots of happy new roles: wife, mom, mother-in-law, stepmom, and grandmother. I also support my husband, Greg, in his literary business with editing, client support, and hostessing.

Because of these wonderful changes and the time it takes to be available to my family, I rarely do public speaking. However, if you need a good speaker for your event, may I recommend my good friends Gene and Carol Kent at Speak Up Speaker Services? They can be contacted at www.speakupspeakerservices.com.

For updates on my books and other news or information visit me at

It's Fun to Be Your Friend

When lives intersect and a bond between women is formed, the treasures of faithfulness, loyalty, and authenticity are discovered. Becky reflects on all these gifts and more as she shares joy-filled stories about how a cherished friend knows us better than we know ourselves, extends forgiveness and grace, believes in our goodness and gifts, offers silence or conversation when we need it, and becomes a reflection of unconditional love.

It's Fun to Be Your Sister

In this gathering of delightful stories about the connection between sisters and sisters-of-the-heart, each engaging chapter reveals why a sister is the gift that keeps on giving. Women with sisters are able to laugh more at life and at themselves, rest in what they have in common, find blessings and inspiration in each other, walk through life with joy and laughter, and share the biggest trials and the simplest pleasures.

It's Fun to Be a Mom

Becky invites women to take a break, catch their breath, and savor stories of pure joy about the privilege, the labor, and the gift of motherhood. These engaging, short tales lead moms to embrace the habits of highly real moms, the strange miracle of breast feeding, the loss of brain cells when one gains a child, the quest for sleep and romance after kids, and the amazing strength of their own mothers.

It's Fun to Be a Grandma

A grandma is to be revered and celebrated. And Becky does just that with stories from her life as a granddaughter and grandmother. With warmth, insight, and her trademark humor, Becky lifts up these special women who believe wholeheartedly in their children and grandchildren, become the keeper of stories and memories, have incomparable strength of spirit and heart, show the women following them how to live richly, and never tire of talking to or about their grandbabies.